Jr. Graphic Biographies™

CHRISTOPHER COLUMBUS
and the Voyage of 1492

Dan Abnett

PowerKiDS press

New York

Published in 2007 by The Rosen Publishing Group, Inc.
29 East 21st Street, New York, NY 10010

Copyright © 2007 by The Rosen Publishing Group, Inc.

First Edition

Editors: Joanne Randolph and Nel Yomtov
Book Design: Julio Gil
Illustrations: Q2A

Library of Congress Cataloging-in-Publication Data

Abnett, Dan.
  Christopher Columbus and the voyage of 1492 / Dan Abnett.— 1st ed.
    p. cm. — (Jr. graphic biographies)
  Includes index.
  ISBN (10) 1-4042-3390-3 (13) 978-1-4042-3390-4 (lib. bdg.) —
ISBN (10) 1-4042-2143-3 (13) 978-1-4042-2143-7 (pbk.)
  1. Columbus, Christopher—Travel—Juvenile literature. 2. America—Discovery and exploration—Spanish—Juvenile literature. 3. Explorers—America—Biography—Juvenile literature. 4. Explorers—Spain—Biography—Juvenile literature. I. Title. II. Series.
  E118.A26 2007
  970.01'5092—dc22

                                        2005037161

Manufactured in the United States of America

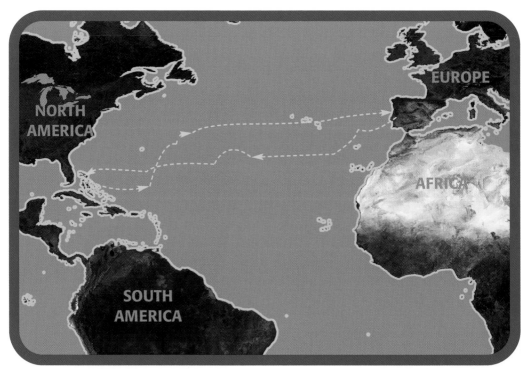

Christopher Columbus's first voyage to the New World

CONTENTS

MAIN CHARACTERS

Christopher Columbus (1451–1506) Master sailor and explorer who crossed the Atlantic Ocean in 1492, hoping to find a water route to Asia. Columbus made three more journeys to the Americas and helped open the way for European exploration of the area.

King Ferdinand (1452–1516) King of Spain who ruled with Queen Isabella. Ferdinand helped make the decision to allow Columbus's trip because it would spread Christianity and give Spain a chance to explore new areas. He and Isabella married in 1469.

Queen Isabella (1451–1504) Isabella supported Columbus's plans to make a journey across the Atlantic. She helped Columbus get the money he needed to make his journey. She also helped make the plans for it.

Martín Pinzón (c. 1442–1493) Pinzón was the captain of the *Pinta*, one of the three ships that Columbus used on his first journey. Pinzón left Columbus during the trip and made discoveries of land and gold on his own. He died soon after he returned to Spain.

Vicente Pinzón (c. 1451–c. 1523) Martín Pinzón's brother, Vicente Pinzón was the captain of the *Niña* during Columbus's first journey. He remained faithful to Columbus.

CHRISTOPHER COLUMBUS AND THE VOYAGE OF 1492

CHRISTOPHER COLUMBUS WAS BORN IN GENOA, ITALY, IN 1451. HE LOVED THE OCEAN SO HE BECAME A SAILOR.

IN 1476, COLUMBUS WAS **SHIPWRECKED** OFF THE COAST OF PORTUGAL. HE MADE HIS HOME THERE.

FOR MANY YEARS TRADERS IN EUROPE HAD REACHED ASIA BY TRAVELING EAST ACROSS LAND.

CHRISTOPHER COLUMBUS BELIEVED HE COULD REACH ASIA BY SAILING WEST ACROSS THE OCEAN. NO ONE HAD EVER DONE THIS BEFORE.

IN 1484, COLUMBUS ASKED JOHN II, KING OF PORTUGAL, FOR THE MONEY AND SHIPS HE NEEDED FOR A **VOYAGE** TO ASIA. THE KING REFUSED HIS REQUEST.

COLUMBUS MOVED TO SPAIN TO RAISE THE MONEY HE NEEDED. AFTER SIX YEARS, KING FERDINAND AND QUEEN ISABELLA FINALLY APPROVED HIS REQUEST IN 1492.

AT LAST! MY DREAM OF FINDING A WATER **ROUTE** TO ASIA IS WITHIN MY REACH! SOON WE WILL SET SAIL!

ON AUGUST 3, 1492, COLUMBUS'S SHIP, THE SANTA MARÍA, SET SAIL FROM THE PORT OF PALOS, SPAIN. THERE WAS A CREW OF ABOUT 40 MEN ON BOARD.

THERE WERE ALSO TWO SMALLER SHIPS SAILING WITH THE SANTA MARÍA. THEY WERE THE NIÑA AND THE PINTA.

MARTÍN PINZÓN WAS THE CAPTAIN OF THE PINTA. HIS BROTHER, VICENTE, WAS THE CAPTAIN OF THE NIÑA.

WE FINALLY BEGIN OUR GREAT VOYAGE!

COLUMBUS'S SHIPS HEADED SOUTH TO THE CANARY ISLANDS. THESE ISLANDS ARE OFF THE COAST OF WESTERN AFRICA.

CAPTAIN, THE *PINTA* IS TELLING US THAT SHE HAS A PROBLEM.

THE *PINTA* DOCKED IN THE CANARY ISLANDS TO HAVE HER **RUDDER** FIXED.

THE *PINTA* IS FINALLY READY TO SAIL, BUT THERE ARE NO WINDS.

COLUMBUS'S SHIPS SAT IN THE CALM WATERS OFF THE COAST OF THE ISLAND.

ON SEPTEMBER 6, THE SMALL **FLEET** FINALLY SET SAIL FROM THE CANARY ISLANDS.

AT FIRST THE WINDS WERE WEAK AND THE SHIPS SAILED SLOWLY.

WE SAIL DUE WEST TO SEARCH FOR CATHAY!*

* CATHAY WAS ANOTHER NAME FOR CHINA.

THE SANTA MARÍA, THE PINTA, AND THE NIÑA SAILED INTO THE ATLANTIC OCEAN.

LIFE ON BOARD WAS HARD. MEN ATE AND SLEPT ON THE OPEN DECK.

THE OCEAN IS SO BIG. WE MAY NEVER SEE LAND AGAIN.

THE FLEET CROSSED A **DANGEROUS** AREA IN THE ATLANTIC OCEAN CALLED THE SARGASSO SEA. ITS WATERS WERE THICK WITH **SEAWEED**.

THE SEAWEED WILL TRAP US!

SOON, HOWEVER, THE TERRIFIED CREW SAILED THROUGH THE DANGER.

THE MEN WERE SCARED AND ANGRY THAT COLUMBUS STILL HAD NOT FOUND LAND.

IF WE DON'T TURN FOR HOME, WE'LL BE LOST FOREVER!

WE WILL SEE LAND SOON! WE CANNOT GIVE UP!

LAND!

ON OCTOBER 12, 1492, THE LOOKOUT SPOTTED LAND.

I KNEW IT! WE HAVE REACHED ASIA!

COLUMBUS BELIEVED HE HAD SAILED ALL THE WAY TO JAPAN, WHICH HE KNEW AS CIPANGO.

COLUMBUS HAD ACTUALLY ARRIVED IN THE BAHAMAS, IN THE CARRIBEAN SEA.

I CLAIM THIS LAND IN THE NAME OF SPAIN!

THIS IS A BEAUTIFUL PLACE, BUT IT IS NOT CIPANGO.

ON OCTOBER 14, THE FLEET LEFT THE BAHAMAS IN SEARCH OF JAPAN.

INSTEAD COLUMBUS LANDED IN CUBA. THE FRIENDLY **NATIVE** PEOPLE HELPED HIM **EXPLORE** THE ISLAND.

THE NATIVES WEAR GOLD.

IF WE WERE TO FIND GOLD HERE, MY MEN AND I COULD BECOME RICH!

WE HAVE SEARCHED THIS LAND BUT STILL HAVE NOT FOUND THE GOLDEN CITIES OF ASIA.

DON'T BE **DISCOURAGED**, MARTÍN. WE MUST KEEP LOOKING.

MARTÍN PINZÓN HAD HIS OWN PLAN, THOUGH.

THE NATIVES HAVE TOLD ME OF AN ISLAND WHERE THERE IS MUCH GOLD. WE WILL SAIL TO THE ISLAND SOON.

MARTÍN PINZÓN TOOK THE PINTA AND LEFT CUBA ON NOVEMBER 22, 1492.

COLUMBUS CONTINUED HIS VOYAGE OF DISCOVERY AROUND THE ISLAND OF CUBA.

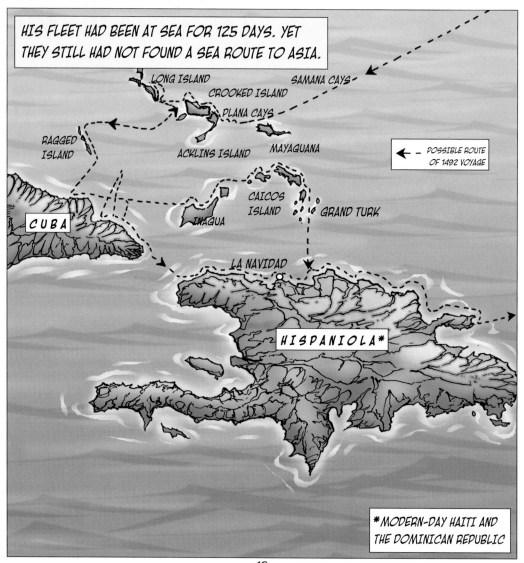

HIS FLEET HAD BEEN AT SEA FOR 125 DAYS. YET THEY STILL HAD NOT FOUND A SEA ROUTE TO ASIA.

LONG ISLAND

SAMANA CAYS

CROOKED ISLAND

PLANA CAYS

RAGGED ISLAND

ACKLINS ISLAND

MAYAGUANA

← — POSSIBLE ROUTE OF 1492 VOYAGE

CUBA

INAGUA

CAICOS ISLAND

GRAND TURK

LA NAVIDAD

HISPANIOLA*

*MODERN-DAY HAITI AND THE DOMINICAN REPUBLIC

ON DECEMBER 5, 1492, THE SANTA MARÍA AND THE NIÑA SAILED EAST FOR THE ISLAND OF HISPANIOLA.

THE SAILORS TRADED SIMPLE OBJECTS FOR GOLD WITH THE NATIVES.

THE NATIVES SAY THERE IS EVEN MORE GOLD TO BE FOUND ON THE ISLAND.

THE SANTA MARÍA AND THE NIÑA SET SAIL ON DECEMBER 24, 1492. THEY WERE SOON IN TROUBLE.

THERE WERE MANY **CORAL REEFS** AROUND THE ISLAND.

THE BOTTOM OF THE SANTA MARÍA WAS RIPPED OPEN ON THE CORAL.

HOW WILL WE RETURN HOME NOW? THE *SANTA MARÍA* IS DOOMED, AND THE *NIÑA* IS TOO SMALL TO CARRY US ALL.

COLUMBUS'S MEN USED THE WOOD FROM THE SANTA MARÍA TO MAKE A **FORT** ON HISPANIOLA.

COLUMBUS CALLED THE FORT LA NAVIDAD.

THE MEN WILL BE SAFE HERE WHILE I RETURN TO SPAIN.

I WILL SAIL HOME TO SHOW THE KING AND QUEEN THE GOLD AND THE PEOPLE I HAVE FOUND HERE.

ON JANUARY 4, 1493, COLUMBUS SET SAIL FOR SPAIN IN THE NIÑA. HE COULD TAKE ONLY A FEW MEN WITH HIM. HE TOOK SOME OF THE NATIVE PEOPLE WITH HIM, TOO.

COLUMBUS LEFT 40 MEN BEHIND AT LA NAVIDAD.

I WILL RETURN SOON AND BRING YOU ALL HOME!

I HAVE ONLY ONE SMALL SHIP AND THE OCEAN IS A DANGEROUS PLACE. WE MUST ALL PRAY THAT WE WILL RETURN HOME SAFELY.

THE NIÑA TRAVELED EAST FOR TWO DAYS, FOLLOWING THE COAST OF HISPANIOLA.

ON JANUARY 6, 1493, THEY SPOTTED ANOTHER SHIP.

SHIP! SHIP!

PINZÓN! IT'S GOOD TO SEE YOU! WE CAN RETURN TO SPAIN TOGETHER!

COLUMBUS HAD BEEN ANGRY WITH MARTÍN PINZÓN FOR LEAVING. NOW HE WAS HAPPY TO HAVE A SECOND SHIP FOR THE JOURNEY TO SPAIN.

THE TWO SHIPS LEFT THE SAMANÁ BAY OF HISPANIOLA 10 DAYS LATER.

THE JOURNEY IS PASSING WELL. THE STARS ARE SHOWING ME THAT WE ARE TRAVELING EAST TOWARD SPAIN.

YET I FEAR THAT THE OCEAN MUST BE THE MOST DANGEROUS PLACE IN THE WORLD.

ON FEBRUARY 14, 1493, THERE WAS A HUGE STORM IN THE MIDDLE OF THE ATLANTIC OCEAN.

DURING THE STORM, THE TWO SHIPS BECAME SEPARATED.

THE NEXT DAY, WHEN THE STORM WAS OVER, COLUMBUS LOOKED OUT ACROSS THE OCEAN.

HE DID NOT SEE THE PINTA, BUT HE DID SEE SOMETHING THAT MADE HIM VERY HAPPY.

LAND! LAND!

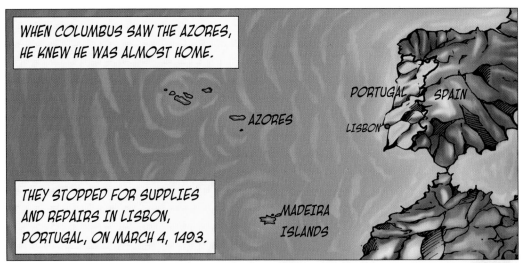

WHEN COLUMBUS SAW THE AZORES, HE KNEW HE WAS ALMOST HOME.

THEY STOPPED FOR SUPPLIES AND REPAIRS IN LISBON, PORTUGAL, ON MARCH 4, 1493.

PORTUGAL   SPAIN

LISBON

AZORES

MADEIRA ISLANDS

COLUMBUS MET WITH PORTUGAL'S KING, JOHN II, TO EXPLAIN HIS JOURNEY.

I HAVE CLAIMED NEW LANDS FOR SPAIN.

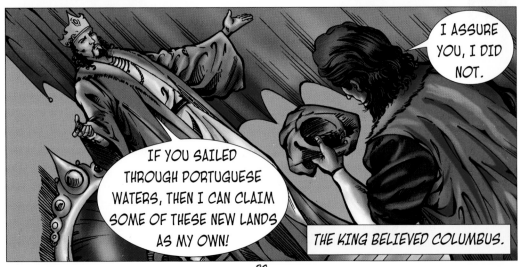

I ASSURE YOU, I DID NOT.

IF YOU SAILED THROUGH PORTUGUESE WATERS, THEN I CAN CLAIM SOME OF THESE NEW LANDS AS MY OWN!

THE KING BELIEVED COLUMBUS.

COLUMBUS REJOINED THE NIÑA AND THEY ARRIVED IN SPAIN ON MARCH 15, 1493.

MY KING AND QUEEN! OUR VOYAGE WAS A SUCCESS!

COLUMBUS'S JOURNEY TOOK 224 DAYS.

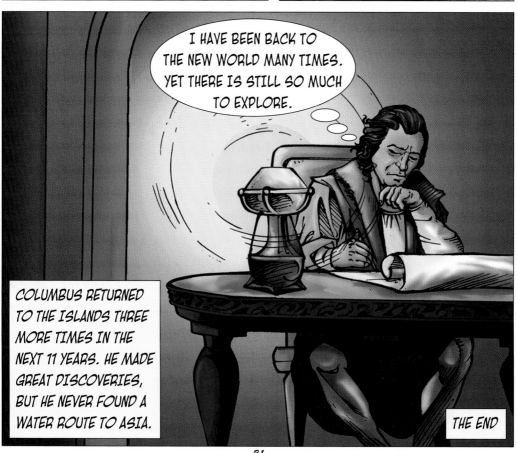

I HAVE BEEN BACK TO THE NEW WORLD MANY TIMES. YET THERE IS STILL SO MUCH TO EXPLORE.

COLUMBUS RETURNED TO THE ISLANDS THREE MORE TIMES IN THE NEXT 11 YEARS. HE MADE GREAT DISCOVERIES, BUT HE NEVER FOUND A WATER ROUTE TO ASIA.

THE END

TIMELINE

1451   Christopher Columbus is born in Genoa, Italy.

1476   Columbus is shipwrecked off the coast of Portugal.

1484   Columbus meets with John II, king of Portugal.

1486   Columbus has his first meeting with King Ferdinand and Queen Isabella of Spain.

1492   On August 3, Columbus sets sail from Palos, Spain, with the *Niña*, the *Pinta*, and the *Santa María*.

On September 6, the fleet sets sail from Gomera, one of the Canary Islands.

On October 12, land is spotted. The fleet has reached the Bahamas. They soon sail to Cuba.

On November 22, Captain Martín Pinzón leaves Cuba in search of gold, against Columbus's wishes.

On December 5, the *Santa María* and the *Niña* sail for Hispaniola.

1493   On January 2, Columbus sets sail on return to Spain.

On January 6, Columbus meets Martín Pinzón off the coast of Hispaniola.

On March 4, Columbus arrives in Lisbon, Portugal.

On March 15, Columbus arrives in Palos, Spain.

GLOSSARY

coral reefs (KOR-ul REEFS) Underwater hills of coral.

dangerous (DAYN-jeh-rus) Able to cause harm.

discouraged (dis-KUR-ijd) To have taken away someone's assurance or certainty.

explore (ek-SPLOR) To travel over little-known land.

fleet (FLEET) Many ships under the command of one person.

fort (FORT) A strong building or place that can be guarded against an enemy.

native (NAY-tiv) Having to do with being born in a certain place or country.

route (ROOT) The path a person takes to get somewhere.

rudder (RUH-dur) A long board that sticks out from the bottom of a ship to steer the ship.

seaweed (SEE-weed) Plants that grow in the ocean.

shipwrecked (SHIP-rekt) Destroyed at sea.

voyage (VOY-ij) A journey, especially by water.

INDEX

WEB SITES
Due to the changing nature of Internet links, the Rosen Publishing Group, Inc., has developed an online list of Web sites related to the subject of this book. This site is updated regularly. Please use this link to access the list:
www.powerkidslinks.com/jgb/columbus/

CAMPUS